Our World

Glass

By Sarah Levete

Aladdin/Watts
London • Sydney

© Aladdin Books Ltd 2005

Designed and produced by
Aladdin Books Ltd
2/3 Fitzroy Mews
London W1T 6DF

**First published in
Great Britain in 2005 by**
Franklin Watts
96 Leonard Street
London EC2A 4XD

A catalogue record for this
book is available from the
British Library.

ISBN 0 7496 6260 3

Printed in Malaysia

Editor:
Harriet Brown

Designers:
Flick, Book Design and Graphics
Simon Morse

Picture Researchers:
Alexa Brown
Fiona Patchett

Literacy consultant:
Jackie Holderness – former Senior
Lecturer in Primary Education,
Westminster Institute,
Oxford Brookes University

Illustrations:
Q2A Creative

Photocredits:
Abbreviations: l-left, r-right, b-bottom, t-top,
c-centre, m-middle
Front cover — Flat Earth. Back cover —
Corbis. 14bl — Astucia. 6bl, 20t, 22bl —
Brand X Pictures. 2-3, 9br, 16t, 17b, 23tr,
28b, 29b — Corbis. 3clt, 3clb, 5tl, 6tl, 9tl,
18t, 24b, 30t — Corel. 3bl, 27bl — Digital
Vision. 19t, 22tr, 28t — Flat Earth. 15tr —
Goredsea.com. 4t, 5bl, 9c, 11tl, 12tl, 13t,
14tr, 18b, 30b — Ingram Publishing. 21t —
NASA. 24tl — Yumi Nozaki (www.yumi-
glass.com). 1, 3tl, 5lc, 5tr, 5br, 15bl, 16b,
17tl, 20b, 26t, 26b, 30c, 31t, 31b —
Photodisc. 4b, 8bl, 10 (both), 12b —
Pilkingtons. 8tl — Rexam. 7tr — Select
Pictures. 11tr, 11c — Courtesy of Wheaton
Village, Millville, NJ, USA.

CONTENTS

Notes to parents and teachers

This series has been developed for group use in the classroom as well as for children reading on their own. In particular, its differentiated text allows children of mixed abilities to enjoy reading about the same topic. The larger size text (A, below) offers apprentice readers a simplified text. This simplified text is used in the introduction to each chapter and in the picture captions. This font is part of the © Sassoon family of fonts recommended by the National Literacy Early Years Strategy document for maximum legibility. The smaller size text (B, below) offers a more challenging read for older or more able readers.

Clear or cloudy?

Glass is useful because it keeps the wind and rain out but lets in sunlight. Glass is naturally transparent.

A

◄ Glass is easy to see through.

Transparent glass is used everywhere, from windows to the glasses that people wear to help them see.

B

Questions, key words and glossary

Each spread ends with a question which parents and teachers can use to discuss and develop further ideas and concepts. Further questions are provided in a quiz on page 30. A reduced version of pages 30 and 31 is shown below. The illustrated 'Key words' section is provided as a revision tool, particularly for apprentice readers, in order to help with spelling, writing and guided reading as part of the literacy hour. The glossary is for more able or older readers. In addition to the glossary's role as a reference aid, it is also designed to reinforce new vocabulary and provide a tool for further discussion and revision. When glossary terms first appear in the text they are highlighted in bold.

See how much you know!

What colour is glass?

Does glass break easily?

What is glass made from?

Is glass always transparent?

Why are other materials added to liquid glass?

What happens to glass that is recycled?

What is a thin thread of glass called?

What do you see in a mirror?

What is special about the glass used in lenses?

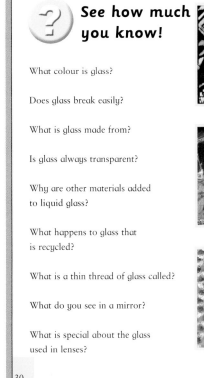

Key words

Crystal

Factory

Light   Liquid

Material   Mirror

Stained   Window

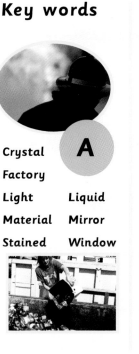

Glossary

Brittle – Something that easily breaks and shatters.
Fibreglass – A material made from tiny threads of glass.
Laminated glass – Strong material made from plastic and glass.
Lens – A curved piece of glass used to help see things more clearly.
Magnify – To make something look bigger.
Mould – A hollow shape.
Obsidian – The natural form of glass.
Opaque – Cloudy, so you cannot see through it clearly.
Optical fibre – A thin glass rod through which flashes of light can pass.
Quarried – Dug out from the ground.
Recycling – To use again and again.

What is glass?

What have a window, a light bulb and a firefighter's clothes got in common? They are all made from glass! This amazing material is all around you. It comes in lots of different shapes and sizes.

◀ **Glass is a very useful material.**

Glass has many special features. Light can shine through glass and you can see through it. It is smooth and colourless. Glass does not let water through – it is waterproof. Glass does not rot or turn rusty. It's easy to make smudges or marks on glass, but it is also easy to clean!

▶ Glass can break easily.

You need to be careful when you touch or hold glass because it can break easily. It is a **brittle** material. Watch out – glass shatters into small sharp pieces that can cut you. Some glass is made so strong that not even fierce winds or heavy hailstones can break it.

People have been making glass for thousands of years!

The first glass objects are over 4,000 years old. They were made in much the same way that we make glass today! During the 14th century, the centre of glass-making was Venice where workers made fine, delicate glass. The workers were punished if they gave away the secret of their glass-making!

 Can you name ten things that are made from glass?

What is glass made of?

Most of the glass that we use is made in a factory. It is made from a mix of sand and other materials. When the mixture is heated, it turns into a thick liquid that looks like see-through treacle. The hot liquid cools down and turns into hard glass.

◀ Glass is made from natural materials.

Glass is made from natural materials – sand, soda and lime. These materials are cheap and plentiful, and found all over the world. They are dug out, or **quarried**, from the ground. Other materials are sometimes used to make certain types of glass. However, sand is usually the main ingredient.

◀ Other materials are added to make special types of glass.

Adding other ingredients to the basic glass mixture makes different types of glass. Coloured glass is made when different chemicals are added to the glass mixture. Thin wires are sandwiched inside a cooling glass mixture to make wire glass which is very strong.

Some natural glass is found in the Earth.

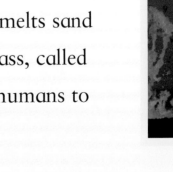

Aztec knife
(700 years old)

Natural glass forms in the mouth of a volcano. The heat of the volcano melts sand and other materials to form natural glass, called **obsidian**. This glass was first used by humans to make very sharp tips for spears!

 Where do the ingredients for making glass come from?

Making glass

Each type of glass is made in a different way. A piece of very thin glass is made in a different way from a strong glass bottle. The liquid glass may be cooled down quickly or slowly to make different kinds of glass. Glass can be shaped in many ways.

◀ Flat, clear glass is called 'float glass'.

In a factory, ingredients are measured and mixed, and then heated up in a furnace (hot oven). As the mixture cools, it is shaped. To make glass for a window, the glass mix is spread over hot liquid metal. It is called float glass because it floats on the liquid metal. The contact between the glass and the metal is perfectly flat.

Glass is shaped when the mix is still runny and hot.

Glass cools quickly so it needs to be shaped before it sets and hardens. Glass can be shaped either by craft workers or special machines.

▲ **You can blow glass up like blowing up a balloon!**

▲ **This bottle was shaped by a mould.**

Liquid glass is poured into a **mould**. As it cools down, air is forced in to make the hollow. The glass hardens and is taken out of the mould.

▲ **Glass-making is skilled work.**

Glass ornaments are often made by heating, joining and shaping several pieces of glass.

 Why can it be difficult to make and shape glass by hand?

Clear or cloudy?

Glass is useful because it keeps the wind and rain out but lets in light. Glass is naturally transparent. This means you can see through it. Glass can be made in beautiful colours. Glass can also be made cloudy so that you can't see through it.

◀ **Glass is easy to see through.**

Transparent glass is used everywhere, from windows to the glasses that people wear to help them see clearly. In the past, some windows were so thick that it was difficult to see through them! Thick glass is less clear than thin glass. Glass that only allows some light to pass through is called **translucent**.

◀ You can't see through some glass!

Some glass only allows through a small amount of light. This cloudy glass is called **opaque**. It is used when people don't want others to see in. Opaque glass is often used on front doors or in bathroom windows.

You can make your own stained glass window!

Collect some coloured sweet wrappers. Ask an adult to help you cut a window frame from black card. Use black sticky tape to stick the wrappers in the window. Put your frame on a windowsill and see the colours as the Sun shines through!

 Where can you see stained glass?

Helpful glass

Imagine your house without glass – it would be very dark with no windows or light bulbs! Today, glass is used for many things from lights to camera lenses. It is even used to make material for clothes. Here we look at ways in which glass helps us.

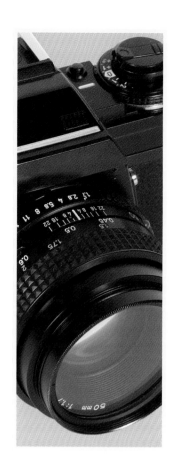

◀ Catseyes® in the road shine in the dark.

In the dark, tiny lights mark out the direction of the road. These lights are made from glass and metal beads. When light from a car shines on them, they reflect the light back and mark the shape of the road. The lights are called catseyes® because they shine in the dark like the eyes of a real cat.

▶ You don't need to dive to see the bottom of the sea!

In some parts of the world, you can take a trip in a glass-bottomed boat. You can look through the glass and see beautiful fish, coral and weird and wonderful plants. The glass is incredibly strong so it doesn't smash and let water into the boat.

Firefighters wear clothes made from fibreglass.

Fibreglass is made from very thin threads of glass. These are thinner than a strand of hair! The fibres can be stuck together with special glue and used to keep warmth in. Firefighters wear fibreglass clothes because they do not catch fire.

Imagine life without glass. How would our lives be different?

Strong glass

If you knock a light bulb it will shatter into tiny pieces. Glass can be very weak or very strong. Some glass shatters easily but glass can also be made strong enough to survive fierce knocks, wild winds and heavy hailstones!

◀ This glass does not fly around when it is smashed.

Laminated glass is made like a sandwich with two layers of glass and a plastic filling. If laminated glass breaks, the pieces of glass stick to the plastic instead of flying around. This kind of glass is used on car windscreens for safety.

◀ This canoe is partly made from glass.

Glass reinforced plastic is strong and hard. It is made by sandwiching glass fibre between layers of plastic. It can be easily shaped and is used to make builders' hard hats, boats and the bodies of some cars and aeroplanes.

This rocket has a glass nose!

When a space rocket blasts into space, it gets extremely hot. Many materials crack at such temperatures. A special glass called glass-ceramic can survive these temperatures without damage. The tops of most electrical ovens are now made of glass-ceramic. Glass-ceramic was actually discovered when glass was overheated by mistake!

 Where else is strong glass needed?

Glass and heat

Glass can keep heat inside a building. A glass greenhouse lets in the Sun's heat to help plants grow. Double glazing can help to keep a house warm. A layer of fibreglass padding can be put in the loft or attic of a house. It keeps the house warm in winter.

◀ **Some glass does not crack when heated.**

The glass in this lantern is heat-resistant. You may have heat-resistant glass jugs, bowls or dishes in your kitchen. Ordinary glass cracks and breaks if boiling water is poured in or put over heat. Glass made with a special chemical does not break when heated. This is useful for glass cooking pots.

▶ Mirrored windows help save energy.

Mirrored glass reflects a lot of the Sun's rays and can stop buildings in hot countries from getting too hot. Double glazing and fibreglass are used to keep houses cool in hot weather and warm in cold weather.

Silvered glass
inner bottle

Silvered glass
outer bottle

Hot or
cold drink

Strong
outer
casing

A thermos® flask keeps your drink hot or cold.

Glass is used inside a thermos® flask. A drink is poured inside a glass container. The glass inside is covered with silver to stop warmth or coldness escaping. Another silver glass layer stops any coldness or warmth entering the thermos® flask.

 What would happen if you dropped a thermos® flask?

Glass for seeing

Do you wear glasses, or have you ever used a magnifying glass to see a tiny insect? Special pieces of glass are used to help us see more clearly. They are very clear and are made in a curved shape. They are called lenses. Glass lets us see images of ourselves as well.

◄ Some glass can make tiny things look bigger.

Look at a bug under a **magnifying** glass and it will look much bigger! The glass used in microscopes and magnifying glasses is called optical glass. Rays of light pass through the optical glass of the **lens** in such a way that it makes the image look bigger. This is called magnifying.

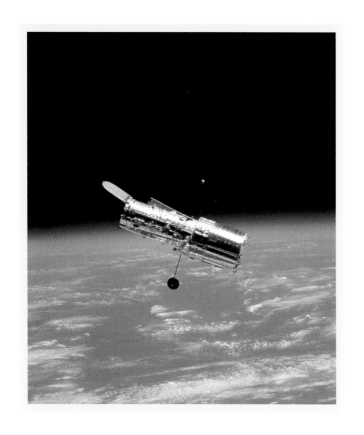

◀ Glass in telescopes helps you see far away into space.

Telescopes help us see things that are far away. Special optical glass lenses or mirrors in telescopes gather lots of light. This brings the picture of faraway stars and planets closer to your eyes.

What do you see in the mirror?

Take a look at yourself in a mirror. Mirrors are made of very shiny glass and have a layer of silver on one surface. Mirrors send back lots of light to your eyes. This lets you see a reflection of what is facing the mirror.

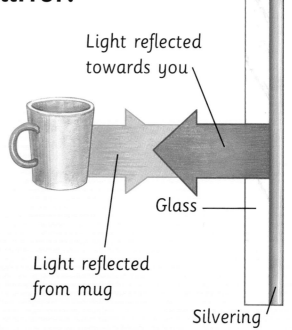

Mirror

Light reflected towards you

Glass

Light reflected from mug

Silvering

 Why can it be useful to see tiny things clearly?

Special glass

Have you ever wondered how your computer works? The answer is with the help of glass! Pieces of glass can be made into tiny threads, thinner than a single piece of hair. These are used to send messages between some computers and telephones.

◀ **Thin pieces of glass can send messages.**

Glass can be made into an **optical fibre**. This is a rod made of a very thin glass tube, coated in a layer of plastic. Lots of fibres are bundled together in cables. The fibres send light messages and pictures around corners. Flashes of light pass down the optical fibre. These flashes of light are like a code.

Glass helps doctors see inside a person's body.

Optical fibres can carry lots of information, and work very quickly. They are used in special medical instruments that help doctors look inside a person's body. These instruments are called endoscopes.

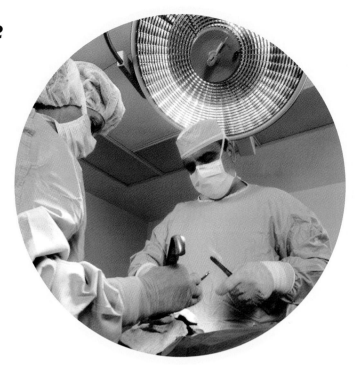

Light in

Outer coating

Light out

This picture shows light going through a glass fibre.

The inside of an optical fibre acts like a perfect mirror. When light enters the fibre, it is reflected many times inside the fibre. In this way, the light is carried up to 100 kilometres in a single optical fibre. That's further than crossing the English Channel to France, and back!

 Can you think why glass is important for the internet?

Beautiful glass

Glass is not only useful. Glass can be made into works of art. It can be turned into beautiful shapes, patterns and colours. Words can be written on glass using tiny drills. It takes great skill to make, cut and pattern glass, without breaking it!

◀ Crystal glass sparkles in the light.

Have you ever seen a glass that seems to sparkle in the light? This glass is called crystal glass. To make crystal glass, a metal called lead is added to the liquid glass mixture. When the glass sets, craft workers can cut tiny shapes into the crystal glass.

◀ You can cut patterns into glass.

An artist uses a small drill to draw patterns on glass. This is called engraving. To write on glass, the artist draws letters with a thin needle. A chemical is used to carve the shape more deeply into the glass. This is called etching.

Turn a jam jar into a beautiful vase.

Ask an adult to help you make a vase. Take care – glass breaks easily and is sharp. You need a clean empty jam jar, paints and a paintbrush. Put your jar on an old newspaper. Carefully paint a pattern on the jar. Leave the paint to dry. Varnish over the paint – you have a beautiful vase.

 Can you think of any glass objects that are useful and beautiful?

Recycled glass

Your glass milk bottle may be made from old glass! Much of the glass we use is made from glass that was used before. Old glass can be melted down and made into new glass. Glass is one of the easiest materials to re-use. This is called recycling.

◀ **Recycle glass to help care for our planet.**

We need to **recycle** glass to save energy. It uses up lots of energy to dig sand, limestone and soda from the ground and take them to factories around the world to make glass. But broken glass, called cullet, melts to form new glass. It uses up less energy and fewer resources than making new glass.

Different colours of glass are recycled separately.

If you go with your parents or carers to the recycling bins, make sure you do not mix different coloured glasses in the same bin. Different ingredients are used to make different coloured glass so they must be kept separate.

A glass bottle is broken, melted and reshaped into a brand new bottle.

Bottles and jars are collected from bottle banks and taken to a glass recycling plant. They are crushed into cullet. Paper and other packaging is taken off the cullet. The cullet is mixed with soda, sand and limestone, heated in a furnace and shaped into a new glass object.

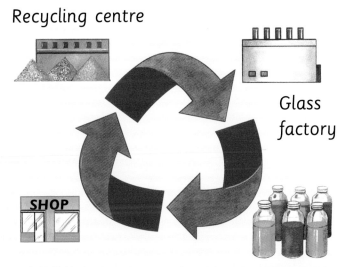

Recycling centre

Glass factory

SHOP

New bottles are filled

 What happens to glass if we don't recycle it?

A glassy future

Today, some glass is mixed with other materials to make it lighter and stronger. Lighter glass is better for our world as it uses up fewer materials. Also, less energy is used to make modern lightweight glass. New types of glass are still being invented.

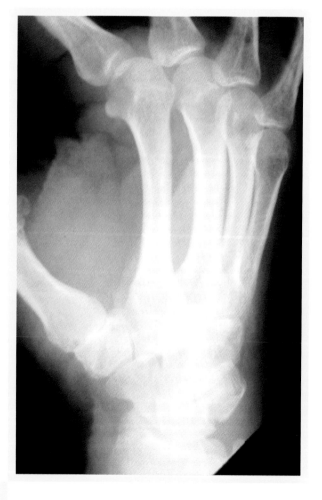

◀ **Glass can help mend human bones.**

Bioglass® is a new material made partly from glass. It contains a substance, called calcium, that is found in bones. Bioglass® can be put inside a person's body. It melts or dissolves and joins onto bones in the body. Bioglass® can help mend and strengthen bones.

◀ Not all glass feels hard.

Foam glass is made by trapping gas bubbles in powdered glass. This makes a spongy material that can protect objects against the cold. Water glass is a powder. It dissolves in water to make a varnish. Water glass doesn't burn. It can make paper fireproof!

Glass can be made in space.

Scientists have discovered that making glass in space creates a very pure glass. Some scientists think they could heat up 'moon dust' and materials from other planets to make a type of space glass. This could be very useful if humans build on a distant planet in the future.

 Can you think of any ways glass may be used in the future?

See how much you know!

What colour is glass?

Does glass break easily?

What is glass made from?

Is glass always transparent?

Why are other materials added
to liquid glass?

What happens to glass that
is recycled?

What is a thin thread of glass called?

What do you see in a mirror?

What is special about the glass
used in lenses?

Key words

Crystal	**Energy**
Factory	**Firefighter**
Light	**Liquid**
Material	**Mirror**
Stained	**Window**

Glossary

Brittle – Something that easily breaks and shatters.

Fibreglass – A material made from tiny threads of glass.

Laminated glass – Strong material made from plastic and glass.

Lens – A curved piece of glass used to help see things more clearly.

Magnify – To make something look bigger.

Mould – A hollow shape.

Obsidian – The natural form of glass.

Opaque – Cloudy, so you cannot see through it clearly.

Optical fibre – A thin glass rod through which flashes of light can pass.

Quarried – Dug out from the ground.

Recycling – To use again and again.

Translucent – Something that is a little cloudy, but you can still see through it.

Transparent – See-through.

Index